Tobey

ABRAMS/MERIDIAN MODERN ARTISTS

Wieland Schmied

Tobey

Harry N. Abrams book for Meridian Books

The Abrams/Meridian Modern Artists Series is published by
Harry N. Abrams, Inc., and distributed by
The World Publishing Company, New York
Standard Book Number: 8109-2100-6
Library of Congress Catalogue Card Number: 66-15214
Printed and bound in Japan

What do we know of Mark Tobey? He has already become a legend, a fabled figure of modern painting, a myth. He has been called "the sage from Seattle," "the sage from Wisconsin," "a wandering mystic." All kinds of nebulous terms have been used in an effort to define his character and the meaning of his works, if not exactly, at least as clearly as possible. A Pacific School of painting has even been discovered, a Northwestern School of the New American Painting, with Tobey at its head. Such a school has never really existed, but the term underscores the extent of his influence and its enduring quality.

Defining Tobey's artistic place is difficult for many reasons. Tobey has always been very reserved. When his international reputation began to grow, shortly after 1950, he was already over sixty years old, with white hair and a white beard—a stately, patriarchal figure, a man of whom little was known and who spoke little about himself. Introspective, unmarried, a "loner," he rarely took part in the bustle of the avant-garde art world, whether in Paris, New York, or Chicago. Indeed, Tobey has preferred out-of-the-way places, such as Dartington Hall in Devonshire; a Zen monastery in Kyoto; and often returns to Seattle, where his style and special insight were formed. He has traveled much—in Mexico, in China, in Europe, in Palestine on a pilgrimage to the holy places of Bahai—a man born in a small town in the Midwest, brought up in the country, fascinated and bewildered by the press of great cities and always searching for the peace of childhood and the worlds of art.

Tobey's extensive travels and his familiarity with foreign cultures, as well as his adherence to an unusual religious creed, may have contributed to the aura of secrecy which quite early surrounded him. More probably, though, it was his obsessive need to paint and to live for painting only, his belief in the power of art as well as in a celestial world, and his complete and uncompromising dedication to art to the exclusion of all else that made him, in the opinion of many people who met him then, a fascinating figure even in his youth.

This is surprising, for the works which made him famous were only created in relatively late years, as the fruit of a lifetime dedicated to art, as the synthesis of many efforts and experiments. Tobey could wait. He has never tried to force or precipitate matters. He became a leading figure of the avant-garde more through inner necessity than by conscious choice. He was already 45 years old when, in 1935, he painted his first mature pictures. Created in the seclusion of rural England, these paintings constitute the beginning of his real work, pictures in which he conveys the frenzy and tumult of Broadway in terms of an Oriental calligraphy. With these paintings he achieved a universal style in which he was able harmoniously to unite oppositions of form and of spiritual and material perceptions.

What could seem to be farther apart than the Japanese traditions of Zen painting and calligraphy; the experience of the American metropolis; and the surroundings of a rural art school in England? Perhaps it required someone essentially naïve, that is, someone of an incorruptible temperament, so that these oppositions could come together naturally and fit into a picture which never looks forced or willed, but which belongs to the great pictorial experiences and discoveries of our time, perhaps the most important since the art of Cubism. When young Tobey—28 years of age—accepted the teachings of Bahai, that optimistic universalism in which all religions fit harmoniously into one unalterable truth as partial aspects of it, his acceptance already expressed his deeply rooted inclination toward the harmony of the whole. "We are all the waves of one sea," says Tobey, alluding to a doctrine of Bahaullah, the founder of Bahai.

Tobey was born in Wisconsin in 1890. He spent his youth in an untamed countryside along the banks of the Mississippi River, and these origins in the late pioneer life of the Midwest, in the humble circumstances of a farmer and carpenter family, long determined his path. Tobey was not a good student, but he early became interested in art, and, when his family moved near the city, attended Saturday classes at the Art Institute of Chicago. The illness of his father soon forced him to give up these classes, however, and he could only continue his education by studying alone. Tobey earned his living in various ways; he worked as a fashion illustrator and portrait painter, and spent almost half a lifetime teaching painting in Seattle. Late-maturing, hungry for culture, fascinated by the ideal of great painting, he found in teaching an opportunity for finding himself, for concentration, for the possibility of learning in the Augustinian sense: "We learn to do by doing," which he likes to quote. But even teaching art did not completely satisfy him. A restlessness remained, the restlessness of a pioneer of the old frontier days, who cannot settle down anywhere in the world. "I take no fixed position," he says. "That may explain the remark once made by someone while looking at one of my paintings: 'Where is the center?' My paintings belong to the type that do not allow the viewer to rest on anything. He is bounced off it or he has to keep moving with it."

6

At present he lives in Basel, in an old patrician house in the suburb of St. Alban, a Gothic house called *Zur roten Tanne* ("At the Red Pine"). In a house digonally across the street are chambers once used by Jacob Burckhardt. In this corner of the world everything looks as if nothing had changed from time immemorial. Most of the rooms of the house are empty—or almost empty: in the great hall there is a small table and a pair of chairs; in the adjoining workroom, with its fireplace opposite the window, nothing but a grand piano; in the next room, a small old desk with many pigeonholes, a large worktable, a great porcelain stove; in the other rooms—insofar as they are shown to visitors—trunks everywhere, and crates and chests, as though Tobey ware about to pack up and leave, as though he stood on the threshold of a great journey.

Tobey, doubtful, skeptical, and at the same time utterly sure of himself, shows the visitor projects he has lately undertaken, experiments in new techniques, with new materials—tracing through gold foil, monotypes printed from ribbed and porous foam rubber or from pieces of plastic, and work with quick-drying glues. There are imaginary portraits, groups of figures, dancers, actors, heads with monstrous hats, Asian masks, faces, spirits—all in motion, looking as though painted in one spurt, in one color—a brownish violet or a greenish blue—or, as Tobey explains, done from a model in tempera, like a monotype. "I am accused often of too much experimentation," Tobey says, "but what else should I do when all other factors of man are in the same condition? I thrust forward into space as science and the rest do. The gods of the past are as dead today as they were when Christianity overcame the Pagan world. The time is similar, only the arena is the whole world."

Although he says little about Bahai, an unshakable devoutness rings through all he says, the devoutness of a widely traveled, cosmopolitan man, who looks at the world in which he lives from a critical distance. Bahai, a religion which unites all religions, with its sense of the unity of all mankind, has been the polestar and compass by which he has guided himself all his life. But his art, which, since those first *Broadway* paintings, those first "white writings" of 1935—36, has developed continuously and without great breaks, probably owes more to his encounter with the Orient, the spirit of Zen painting, the calligraphic impulse he received in Japan. "Bahai sought me, but I sought Zen," he says.

He places the Japanese aesthetic over the Chinese. More important to him than the handling of brushes and the technique of *sumi* (Japanese ink) painting was his penetration into the world view of the East, the insight into the dynamic character of the world. "Relationships, tensions, are more important than the things they connect," the Japanologist Ernest Fenollosa had already pointed out before the turn of the century. Tobey rediscovered in this the pre-Socratic concept of a constantly changing universe *(panta rei)*, the knowledge that duration and being exist only in the transitory, in change, in repetition. From this we can understand his work, his attempt to reflect the world through the "moving line," the moving, living, animated line. His white writings, his compositions with the moving line, and out of its resulting "moving focus" the variable visual point—though they were created earlier—first became well known simultaneously with action painting and *art informel*, so that it was natural to relate them to postwar trends in art. After winning the gold medal for painting at the Venice Biennale in 1958, he became known in Europe, and at that time the critics called him "an intimate Pollock." This comparison with the younger Jackson Pollock (1912–1956) was meant as praise. If we understand the term correctly, it is supposed to mean something like this: Jackson Pollock succeeded in freeing painting from Constructivist constraint, in raising the value of the gesture and of spontaneity in the act of painting, and in the expression of a new, dynamic space conception. This he achieved and realized on his gigantic canvases, which he approached with the greatest concentration, as though the aim was to triumph over an opponent, and as though the act of painting were a battle with the monster of the empty expanse. All this Tobey achieved and realized, often on a tiny piece of paper, with hair-fine brush, submerged in meditation at his writing table; but instead of using his entire physique, as Pollock did, he uses a delicate stroke, a movement of the hand governed by the wrist, in place of Pollock's impulsive and violent gesture. Thus understood, this analogy is not a bad characterization of Tobey.

And yet, the above is not precisely true. Tobey is not "an intimate Pollock," just as Pollock is not a Tobey in gigantic size: Tobey is Tobey. And, most important, he achieved his result several years earlier, approaching it by different paths and from other premises. Tobey's paintings *Broadway, Broadway Norm,* and the no-longer extant *Welcome Hero* date from 1935 and 1936; anything comparable in form by Pollock, not before 1943. Also, as in Pollock, the influence of Surrealism is unmistakable. (After the German occupation of France during the Second World War many of the most important members of the Surrealist group emigrated to the United States: Max Ernst, Duchamp, Masson, Chagall, Matta, and, most important, their leader and mentor, André Breton. The group settled mainly around New York and its ideas and exhibitions influenced and stimulated many of the artists who were to be in the vanguard of Abstract Expressionism, Tachism, and Action Painting.)

The quieter character of the art of Tobey, who lived in Seattle, behind the barrier of the Rocky Mountains, may explain why Pollock first caught our attention. During 1946 and 1947 Pollock, Arshile Gorky, De Kooning, Hans Hofmann, and Franz Kline were the leading spirits of the New York avant-garde, which at that time was considered extreme. Or perhaps it is simply that Tobey was always a solitary, and so (however much or little he may have influenced the mainstream of contemporary art) his work can by the very nature of things only be classified in retrospect, when we are no longer confused by other movements and artistic trends. Tobey has never belonged to a "school"; the often cited Pacific School in which, besides Tobey, the painting of Graves, Anderson, Callahan, and others are grouped is, in fact, only geographic. Actually, the name designates a group of individualistic painters on the West Coast who did not participate in the developments taking place in New York, but who among themselves held widely divergent artistic positions.

Yet it was in New York and Paris that the decisions were made which led to the international preeminence of a new style of painting. In 1947 the manifesto *Vers l'abstraction lyrique* appeared, on the occasion of the exhibition "L'Imaginaire" at the Galerie de Luxembourg, in which Hartung, Mathieu, Wols, and others participated. In New York, in 1952, Harold Rosenberg coined the term "Action Painters," and in Paris Michel Tapié coined the term *art informel* in 1951 and *un art autre* in 1952. In 1954 Pierre Guéguen spoke for the first time of "Tachism." With this, the conceptual vocabulary with which Tobey's work, too, is customarily described was complete. Tobey's oeuvre, after individual pieces were exhibited in group shows of modern American painting (first at the Tate Gallery in London in 1946, then 1948 in Venice, 1951 in Berlin, 1952 and 1954 in Paris, 1955 in Bern), was first properly documented in one-man shows from 1955 (Paris, Galerie Jeanne Bucher) to 1961 (Paris, The Louvre)—in other words, relatively late. This delay had its good effects, for because of it the significance of Tobey really entered our field of vision at the moment when the high tide of Tachism, which flooded the galleries of Europe with so much flotsam and jetsam, began to ebb. Then we could see, at once, not only the inner relationship which connects Tobey to the masters of *art informel*, but also his considerable differences from them. As a result, when today the once so enthusiastic appraisal of Action Painting, *art informel*, and Tachism is thoroughly revised, the work of Tobey remains unscathed.

One could add here that in the strict sense there has never been an *art informel*. It was informal only if one equates form with geometric, static form. But the great achievement of Pollock and Tobey was that they found a new kind of form, one which no longer breaks up into single, independent forms, but can only be equated with the painting surface seen as an entirety in motion. The individual form, which has a hard outline and can usually be defined geometrically, is somewhat static, immovable; an activation of the picture surface could not develop from these "old" forms. Only a form-continuum created out of a multiplicity of moving form-particles could express the dynamic of a world view of open, vibrating space, which no longer stands in opposition to the form which fills it, but, rather, is itself form. This was something entirely new in the history of art. To Cubism we are indebted for multiplane perspective, the simultaneous view of various sides of one and the same object. Thereby a "one-after-another" in time was turned into a "next-to-each-other" in space, and the opposition between the changeable perception of a thing and its essential nature was overcome. This happened in about 1909 in the paintings of Picasso, Braque, Gris, Léger. A generation later Mark Tobey took a decisive step further.

The dimension of time in a painting had been obvious to him since the late twenties in Seattle, when he made what he calls his "personal discovery of Cubism." By this he meansthat it became obvious to him that a picture requires time, time to unfold, its own kind of time which is different from everyday time, and that a work of art can never be a "snapshot" of reality. But because time and space are inseparable in our perception, that which has to do with our conception of time must also have its effect on our relationship to space.

Therefore it is not the individual object which interests Tobey, and not the perspective in which the world appears to the human eye. Form, object, perspective—for him, all these are in continual motion, and, isolated, are inconceivable. They only become conceivable in a space which is not merely a display area or a container, but is filled with energies, tensions, powers, relationships, wellsprings—a space in which the opposition between object and emptiness no longer exists. It must be an imagined, a sensed space—the space of our consciousness. "The dimension that counts for the creative person is the space he creates within himself. This inner space is much closer to the infinite than the other, and it is the privilege of a balanced mind—and the search for an equilibrium is essential—to be as aware of inner space as he is of outer space."

If one wants to characterize Tobey's work in greater detail, one should perhaps dispense entirely with a vocabulary committed to the trends of modern art, and instead search for the sources which nourished it. These lie in the Far East. In doing this we must rid ourselves of the thought that Tobey simply adopted individual techniques or thematic elements. He himself wrote: "Artistically speaking, I have already had several lives. Some critics have accused me of being an Orientalist and of using Oriental models. But this is not so, for I knew when in Japan and China—as I struggled with their *sumi* ink and brush in an attempt to understand their calligraphy—that I would never be any but the Occidental that I am. But it was there that I got what I call the calligraphic impulse to carry my work on into some new dimensions . . . . With this method I found I could paint the frenetic rhythms of the modern city, the interweaving of lights and the streams of people who are entangled in the meshes of this net." Tobey early grasped America's cultural position between Europe and Asia, and from his first years in Seattle tried to make it fruitful for his work. "If the West Coast had been open to aesthetic influence from Asia, as the East Coast was to Europe, what a rich nation we would be!"

Tobey's achievement can only be understood as the attempt to offer the insights and experiences of the Chinese and Japanese aesthetic to Occidental painting, for the enrichment and renewal not only of the American, but of the European as well, at a time in history when our artists set themselves the task of accepting the influences of all epochs and cultures in order to become truly universal. The role which Tobey has played in the development of a new space conception in modern painting can only be compared to the mediating function Ezra Pound performed for the literature of our century in the disclosure and penetration of Far Eastern figures of speech and principles of form. Pound and Tobey were certainly searching for different things in Asia: Pound for a doctrine of the creative life, the proper way of life in the Confucian sense, the ancient Chinese sense of the State as the harmony of heaven and earth, nature and man, family and the individual. Tobey was searching for the meditative, oriented toward the Beyond, Taoism rather than Confucianism; in Japan he was attracted to the philosophy of Zen rather than the Shinto tradition. And yet, in their feeling for the fleeting, the transitory, the allegorical quality of all appearances, in their understanding of existence, which only unfolds itself in perpetual motion, they are related to each other. Pound succeeded in making the step from image to ideogram, from the poem, which renders a static picture or situation, to the method of the canto, which catches fire from concrete details and made it possible for him to tie together, through typal examples, historically disparate facts, forms, events, the mythical and the present.

What his occupation with the ideographic roots of Chinese characters was to Pound, his meeting with the Chinese student Teng Kwei in 1923 in Seattle was for Tobey. Teng Kwei initiated him into the technique of calligraphy. Everything was set into motion for him. "I need only take one step backward into the past," he later described this discovery, "and the tree in front of my studio in Seattle is all rhythm, lifting, springing upward!" From that point on, the tree and all other objects were no longer static, no longer "solid." Through the "living line" he learned to break up, dissolve, and make the fixed forms transparent for other forms lying behind them, to make the volumes of bodies porous, to open them to the void, to space. His primary interest from then on was line. By renouncing the representation of the perspective three-dimensionality of space, which after all is static, it seemed to him that the space began to live, as though he could touch it. "I developed a sort of sixth sense for space," he said. Now the aim was to go further, to fill the newly won space—with "mass." By this Tobey means the aggregate of his characters, the web of lines often executed on different levels, the sum of the "moving lines," which build up an incorporeal, ethereal substance and bring the space into vibration. He lays many levels over each other—experiences, the trail of the brush, the most delicate strokes, suggestions of forms, signs, gestures—covers them up and knits them into the spiderweb of his lines. By this method he achieves depth, "multiple space," and "moving focus." Multiple space and moving focus in their basic form resulted entirely out of the calligraphic impulse. At first slowly, they resolved themselves out of the objective picture of the street bustle, and in his loveliest paintings they melt, through the lines of the white writing, into an undulating space continuum of boundless freedom, which encloses all time and simultaneously lifts it into a moment of eternity.   12

It was not only calligraphic impulse which Tobey acquired in his meeting with Teng Kwei in Seattle and in the seclusion of the Zen monastery in Kyoto; what he discovered in Far Eastern painting was concentration and consecration as the source and goal of all of man's creativity. This seemed to him to be a confirmation of his deepest conviction, his own interpretation of the meaning of man's existence, and created a bridge for him from Bahai to Zen.

Tobey has a depth of perception, a purity and incorruptibility of feeling, which guided him even in his early years, and which for forty-five years did not permit him to be satisfied with what he did. He sensed that these efforts of his still lacked the decisive factor—complete harmony with his conception of the inner world. This harmony could not be forced, and when it appeared, Tobey felt it to be a gift of grace. Among all the painters of our time, Klee and Feininger were probably the closest to him in this interpretation of art. Lyonel Feininger, whom Tobey often visited in his New York home, and who owned a number of his watercolors, soon recognized the kinship of the man in the artist who was so different from him. He responded to Tobey's comment, that light as a unifying idea guides the picture to peace and freedom, and said: "With an unusual intensity Tobey builds up these worlds of his visions."

Tobey's is a world of hidden relationships, a world of visible order, of heightened consciousness. His paintings are pictures of a lifelong experience of the world, pictures which require an open, wakeful, perceptive eye. He himself says: "Always in movement—that is how the Greek philosophers saw the essential being of the soul—so, I have tried to tear out just a few scraps of that beauty which makes up the miracles of the Cosmos and which is in the multi-facetedness of life."

Illustrations

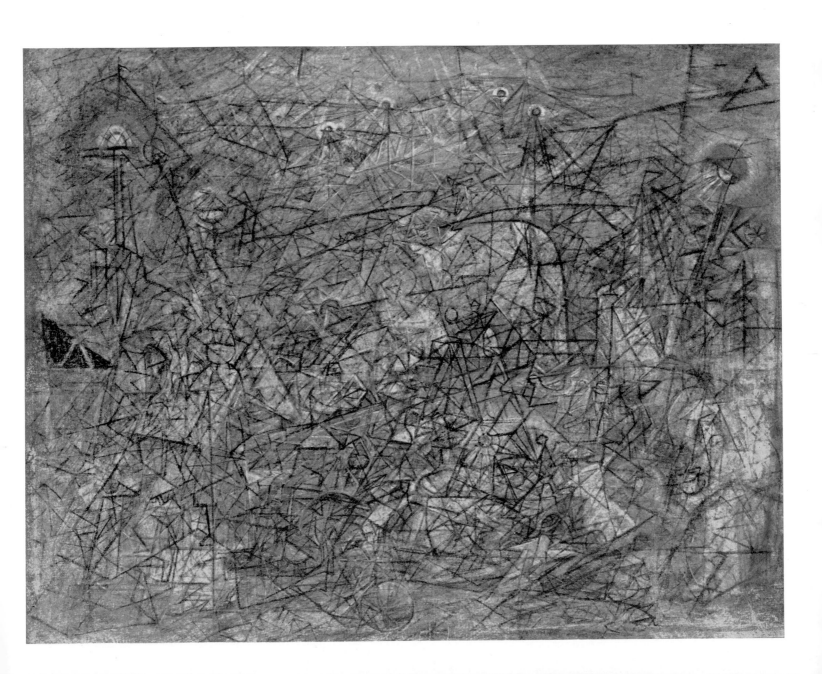

18

24

30

31

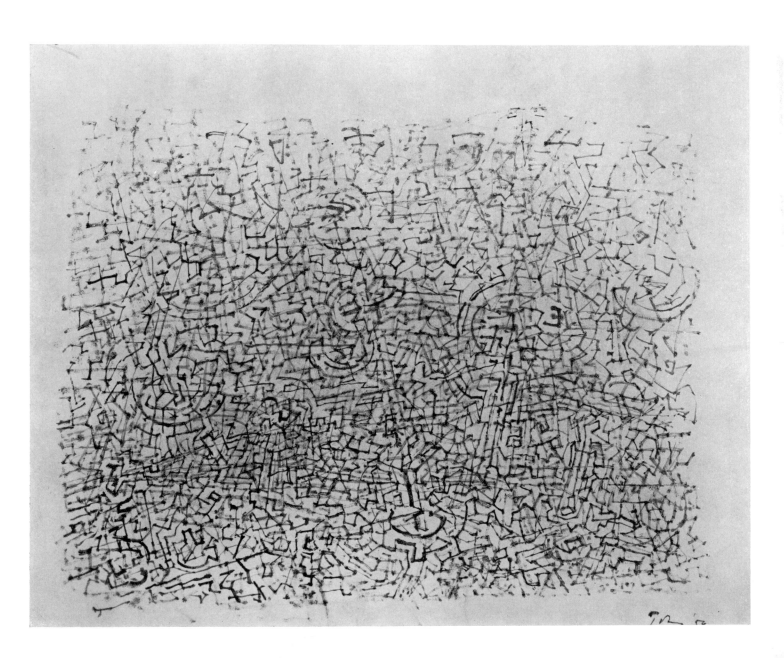

From the "Meditative Series." 1954

Tobey created two related picture series in 1954, as well as many other works. He named the first group *Void*, the other *Meditative Series*. *Void* marks the most radical step that Tobey had taken up until that time. The viewer is confronted with an empty, dark, earth-gray surface; this covers a reddish tone which lies beneath it and tries to push itself toward the surface at various points around the edges. It seems as though the colors of the earth were covered over with a shroud. All is silence. We know the significance the Orientals place on empty spaces in a picture. The emptiness leads not only to contemplation—it also has a creative, evocative power. It denotes the source. In this sense the *Meditative Series* follows upon the pictures of the *Void* for Tobey. The empty spaces now possess magic attraction. They are filled with white writing—countless tiny little white figurations, layered over each other, poured on each other, filling a reddish-brown ground, like footprints on a desert, fossilized traces of an obliterated past. All thought is on the goal, the contradictions resolved. It is a meditation tablet. The eye wanders around on the surface without finding a resting place, yet the viewer is filled with a sense of quiet. Movement turns in on itself. There is peace. William C. Seitz called these small pages of the *Meditations* "visual prayers... profound communions with God, nature, and the self." 34

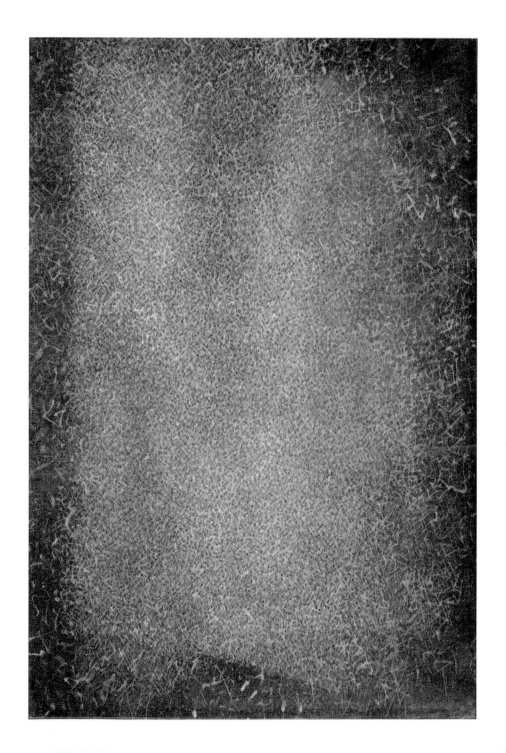

Celestial Concert. 1954

This work was originally titled *Ange*—not *Angel*, for Tobey has an aversion to the word in English, as though it were weighted with unpleasant connotations. But later he discarded this title, perhaps because there is too much restlessness in the painting. It is a concert of many voices, gay and sober, high and deep, calm and aggressive. Its inner dynamism and multiplicity contrast with the quiet monochrome of the *Meditative Series*. Tobey once said that there are really only two distinctive "isms," two spiritual attitudes—Classic and Romantic—and that he felt himself drawn by both at different times. According to him, the inspiration for the *Meditative Series* was Apollonian, that for the city pictures, Dionysian. *Celestial Concert* belongs to the latter group, even though it transposes the city into a divine metropolis. Impressions of great cities appear—abbreviated and cryptic, jumbled up—the letters of neon signs, a maze of people and cars on the streets, but to the experienced eye it appears as a representation of a higher order. The city is a theme which returns in the most varied transmutations and gradations of abstraction from the *Broadway* pictures of 1935 on, a theme which never leaves Tobey. He has thought a great deal about modern architecture and city planning, and holds architects and city planners guilty in part for the ills of modern man ("they have hearts of stone"). About his city paintings he has said: "No doubt I did them because I am an American painter. I cannot be indifferent to the swarming crowds, multitudes, neon signs, movie theaters, to the noises I hate of modern cities." But here the "true essence of tumult and agitation of modern cities" (Lyonel Feininger) is echoed as though freed of all accidentals and seen in some celestial mirror. The tumult is harnessed, the agitation is transformed into organic motion, the noise gives way to the melody of ensemble playing. But nothing is at rest. The colors—from white, through dominant pink, to violet—are active. No fixed point gives the eye pause. One might almost say, to allude once more to the banal terminology of the city theme: it finds no parking place. Pulled into a vortex, all motion distinctly aims toward a center and is then impelled outward, as though—and with this we return to the aural dimension of this complex work—the concert were conducted from this center.

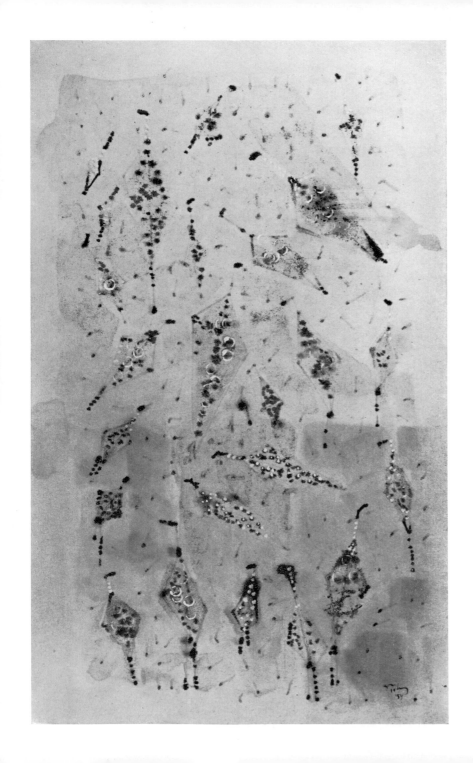

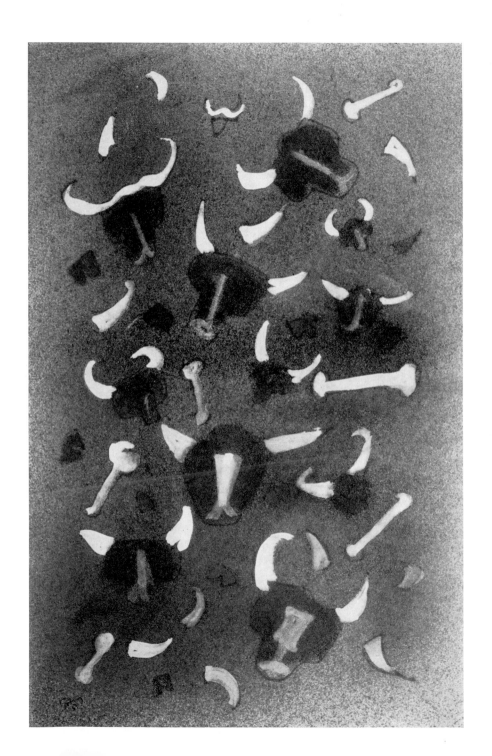

Multiple Voyages. 1957

A classic Tobey painting. Here one sees only the finely brushed white writing over a reddish-brown ground which is left as a border; the white writing is as ephemeral as a breath—a mere thread or trickle of water—laid on a little more heavily in places. A few black characters, here and there, are almost invisible. Although no separate planes are indicated, the picture nonetheless achieves spatial depth and evokes the experiences of a man who has traveled widely and who has been on the move his whole life long. Fragments of the route traced by the delicate brush are overlayered; they are both memories of other journeys and visible traces of the actual physical painting process. The threads intermingle, and if you try to follow a single one, you are led into a labyrinth and lose your way. And yet, out of all the paths together there is created, in memory, a picture of the world.

Southern Sky. 1958

A painting of divine beauty. A painting of remembrance. Here again the optical discoveries of many journeys, the experience of the starry skies above many countries are preserved. Though line dominates in most of Tobey's paintings— that spiderweb of the most delicate brush strokes—here color dominates, in spots and blots and dabs laid on the paper with a soft brush. For Tobey, color is a gift of his late years. For a long time he was afraid of it, and avoided it. He felt it bound him too much to the earthly, and remembered that in the Orient color is considered to be just something for children. The world of color is a happy one, but it is really not a spiritual world, as Persian miniatures, the art of the Fauves, and the pictures of Matisse seemed to prove to him. Because of this, Tobey usually confined himself to tonal values, preferably to a few variations of white. But in this painting, thinking of southern climes, he has for once yielded completely to the seduction of color. The stars sparkle yellow and white in the jeweled heavens.

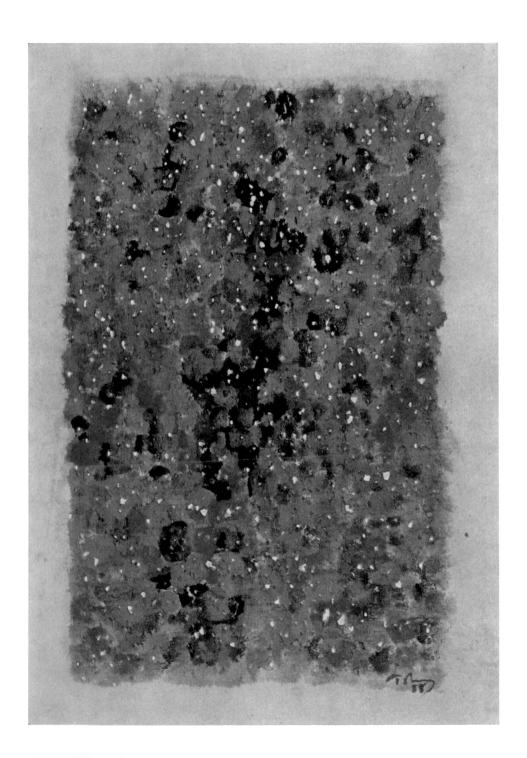

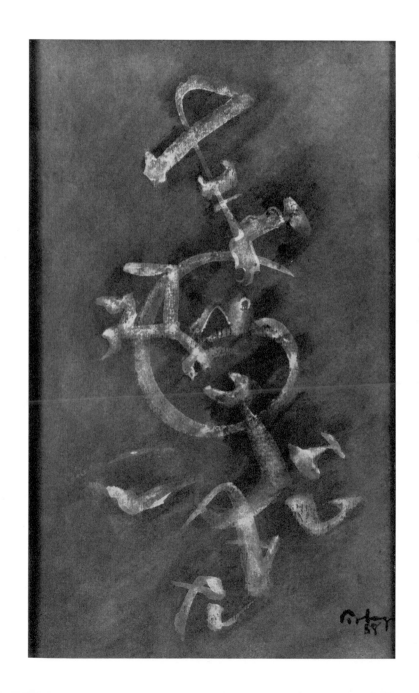

The Old Pond. 1959

A bit of earth, covered with water. Flooded. Is it seen through the naked eye, or perhaps through a microscope? *Old Pond.* The title is not meant to be descriptive, but probably—as with almost all of Tobey's pictures—originated later, an association which appeared when he viewed the interplay of violet-red, brownish green, and grayish yellow. The picture does not represent an actual pond, but is itself—the piece of paper decorated with color—a pond, one which never before existed, and which originated from the observation of many ponds and many other objects in this world. 46

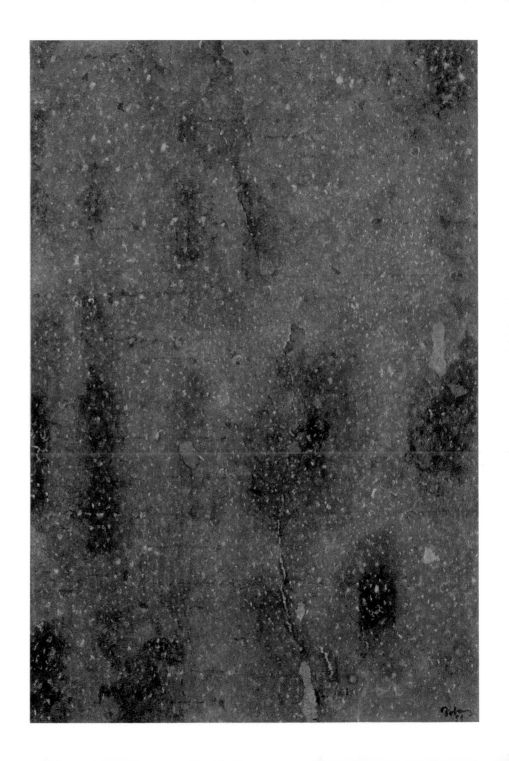

Within Itself. 1959

A calligraphic picture. White, black, violet, gray, and brownish characters intertwine on a bright pink ground. A thick, impenetrable, unified, vibrating surface, but—as is so often the case with Tobey—what depth, how much space it suggests! One seeks vainly to penetrate, to get *behind* the picture, yet ever again becomes caught as though in a tangle of briers and is left hanging, cannot tear loose. The longer one looks, the greater the mystery. Everything turns inward and remains trapped within itself.

Targets. 1959

White characters and red flecks appear on a brown ground which is divided into parts by horizontal darker areas. Calligraphy? Or figures constructed of wire? It is an airy game. The picture is called *Targets.* How can one hit the targets if they keep moving, if they cannot be grasped, like sunbeams dancing on a dark wall? Usually Tobey's white writings are woven into a vibrating web of space. But here individual, archaic figurations seem to float motionless.

Intertwined. 1959

Various characters—snakelike lines, half-moons, dots and swirls—blue, violet, red, and white, some made with a heavier brush, others with a finer one, are all irrevocably interwoven and held together, imprisoned within the dark green border. Lifelines, deathlines, over, under, burrowing, buried . . . swallowed-up threads of a story that has no ending. One thinks of the *no* play *Nishikigi,* which Tobey may have seen in Japan and which Ezra Pound and Ernest Fenollosa translated in *The Classic Noh Theatre of Japan.* The ghost of an unhappy lover says to the ghost of his love, with whom he has not been united:

> Tangled, we are entangled. Whose fault was it, dear? tangled up as the grass patterns are tangled in this coarse cloth, or as the little Mushi that lives on and chirrups in dried seaweed. We do not know where are today our tears in the undergrowth of this eternal wilderness. We neither wake nor sleep, and passing our nights in a sorrow which is in the end a vision, what are these scenes of spring to us? this thinking in sleep of some one who has no thought of you, is it more than a dream? and yet surely it is the natural way of love. In our hearts there is much and in our bodies nothing, and we do nothing at all, and only the waters of the river of tears flow quickly.

52

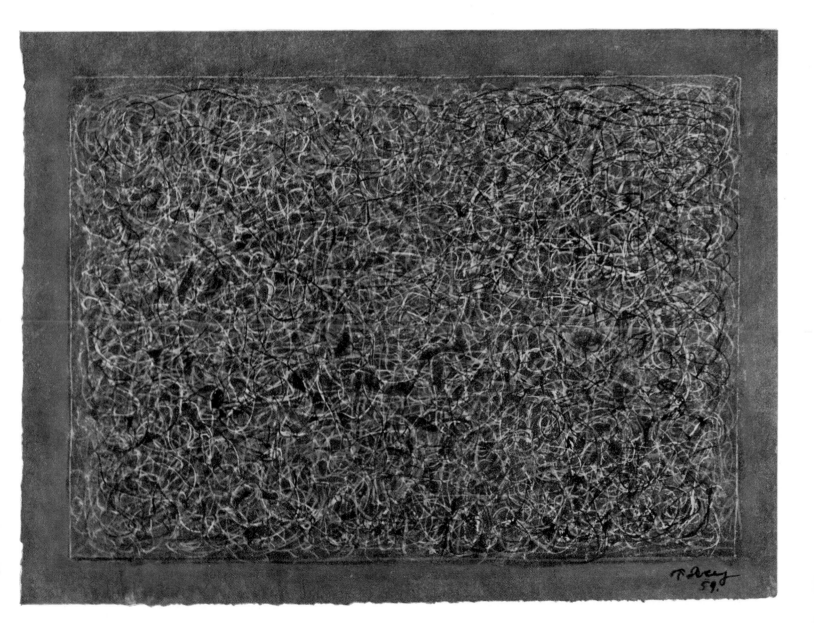

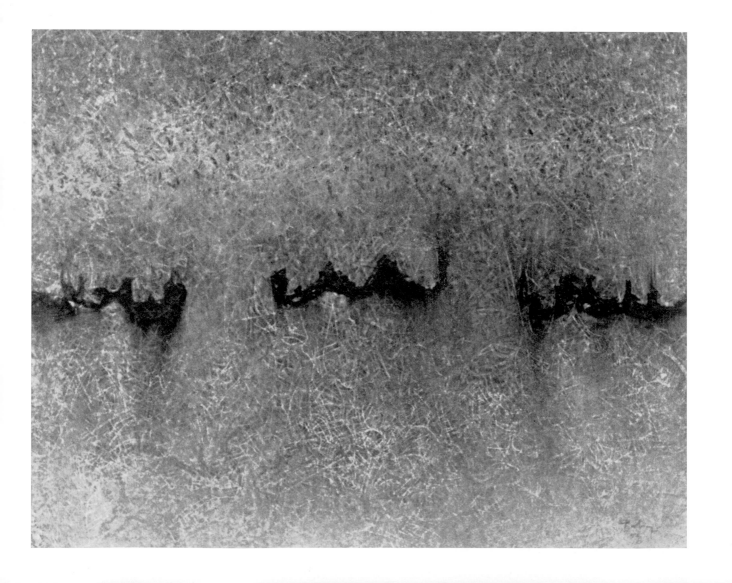

54

Pacific Drift. 1959/62

The title has special meaning for Tobey. For him Seattle, San Francisco, the cities of the Pacific Coast, were America's gateways to the world of the Orient. In Seattle he suddenly became aware of his proximity to the East—just as later, in the solitude of the Zen monastery in Kyoto, he became aware of how much a man of the West he remained. In Seattle he made the acquaintance of Teng Kwei, a young Chinese painter, who introduced him to the Far Eastern approach to art. Later, in "Reminiscence and Reverie," he wrote that in San Francisco he always felt the seething floodtide of the Orient in the great bay. Thus for him the currents of the Pacific bring with them much of Chinese and Japanese tradition, harmonies which we can find in his calligraphic impulse, in the brush stroke, in the delicate colors. 56

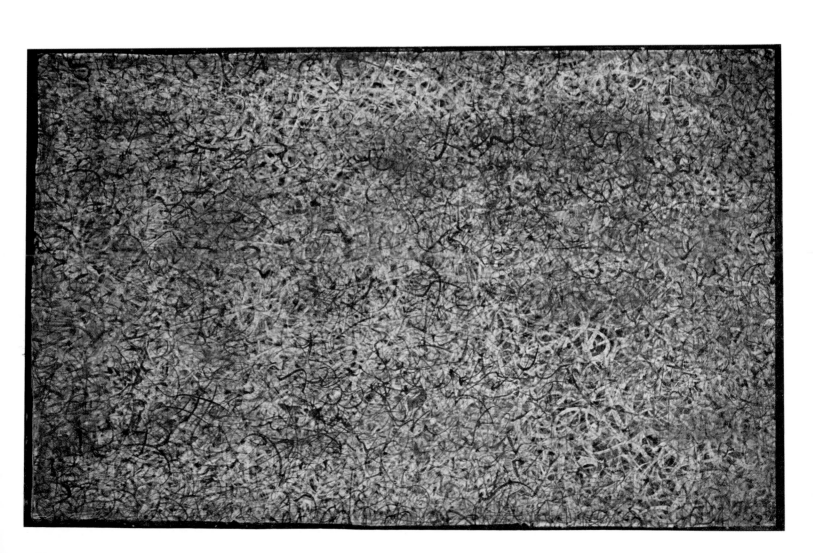

Ritual Fire. 1960

The white writing rises like smoke. Down on the ground a fire seems to burn—the earth glows. The air, brought into motion, swirls, glimmers, pushes upward, and thickens toward the top of the painting. The movement here does not, as in *Celestial Concert,* move toward the center, but strives upward, turns at the top, and crowds along the edge. Tobey's paintings almost never seem to be pieces cut out of a larger whole, nor is their energy dissipated in the space outside of the boundaries, which here are a brownish red. He encloses the picture as in a house, but within this space it glows. We seem to witness a fire dance, a rite. Associations with the primitive world, the art of the Indians (which Tobey collects), and their ritual dances lie close at hand in this work.

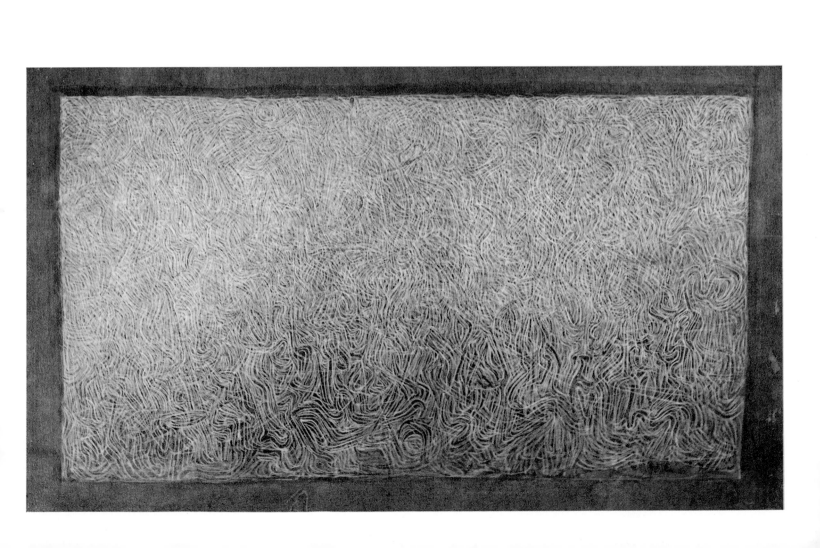

Tumble Weed. 1960

An autumnal painting. Tobey has so often been inspired by autumn foliage, by the veining of a dried leaf, a bent reed, sere grass. A single leaf, in its structural plan, reminds him of all nature. One of his favorite photographs shows him in his house in Basel, sitting with hands entwined at the drawing table, on which lie some brown chestnut leaves. The window looks out on a garden. Perhaps he loves autumn even more than spring, for to the knowing eye the vanished blossom is still implicit in the leafless branch. Tumble weed—wandering grass, breaking from its roots, wind-driven across the fields and prairies—a hopelessly interwoven, rolling mass. Surely it belongs to Tobey's boyhood memories, and surely he was thinking of this helplessly driven quality, of powers outside ourselves, as his brush strokes evolved this restless spinning which stretches from one edge of the picture to the other. Autumn grass in the wind. Are we viewing it from above or from below? From the air or from the floor of the earth? One cannot look for ordinary perspective in this painting, for many viewpoints are united in it, many kinds of space and time. But the main impression is of autumn, of the withered weed, sere and rootlessly driven.

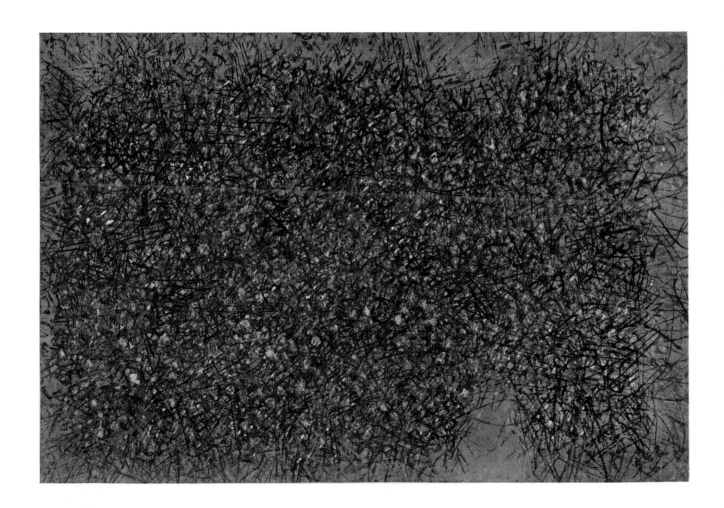

61

Homage to Rameau. 1960

Most of Tobey's pictures are enclosed units which return cyclically into themselves. Their action does not continue beyond the edge of the picture—the movement does not flow on into infinity. Instead, they seem to rise up from great depths—or to reach down into them. This is especially clear in the present instance. Out of the deepest black a deep blue rises up, and out of the deep blue a black writing, and out of the black writing the white one. Usually the writing dominates the color, covers it, buries it. Here color and drawing are in balance. The color glows in full light, and the calligraphy seems to dance on the blue ground, set in musical motion.

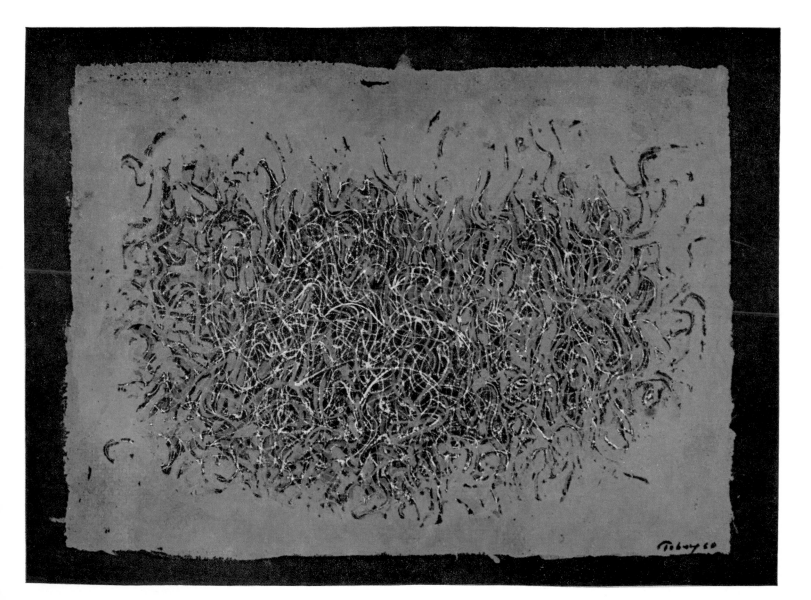

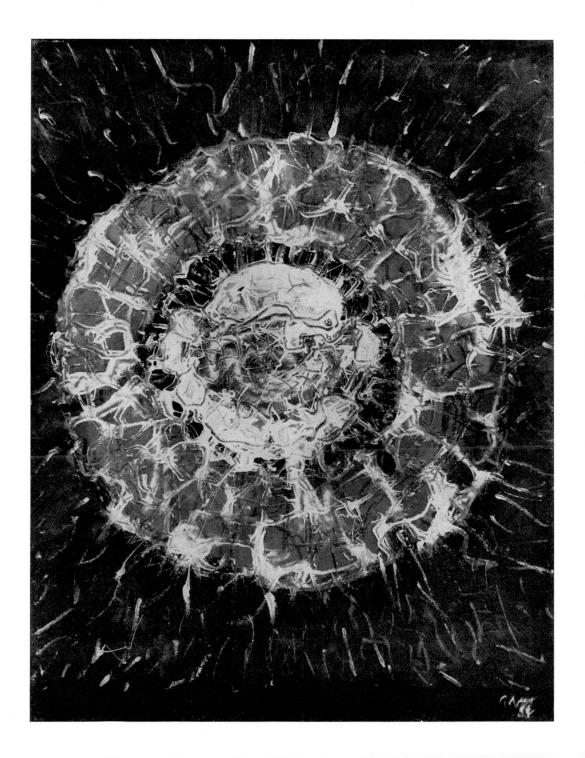

65

Centre agité dominé. 1960

This is a dramatic picture, one that speaks of manifold happenings. The characters are still trembling, as from an earthquake. A crater has burst open, the ground is broken up, and out of the depths confused signs crowd forth like a dark oracle. Tobey has here playfully united several creative methods. The delicate white writing is covered over with pencil strokes. The characters are contrasted with broader brush strokes—crosses, hooks—the gestures of an agitated yet disciplined hand. What we speak of as "gesture" in modern painting plays a very small part in Tobey's work. Here he indicates what a subordinate and controlled function it should have in the picture. Aligning himself with Cézanne, he believes that the painter should not consciously introduce a personal element into the creation of the picture. "Let nature take over in your work," Tobey wrote. "These words from my old friend Takizaki were at first confusing but cleared to the idea: 'Get out of the way.'"

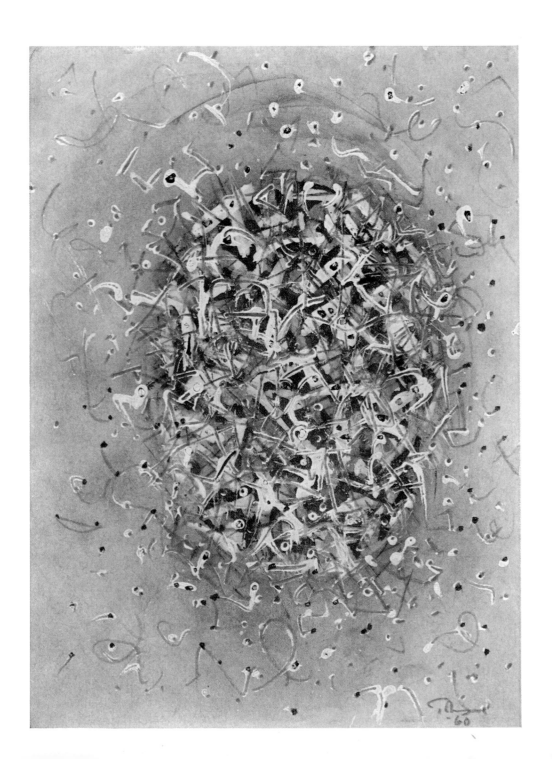

67

Electric Dimensions. 1960

Space, whether physical space or any other kind, is never empty for Tobey. "Scientists say," he told William C. Seitz, then Curator of Painting at the Museum of Modern Art in New York, "that there is no such thing as empty space. It's all loaded with life... teeming with electrical energy, potential sights and silent sounds, spores, seeds, and God knows what all." The space in *Electric Dimensions* is especially filled with energy, with tension, with movement. Lightning seems on the verge of flashing. For Tobey, a deeper problem is buried in all tension and movement—the first and last problem of all painting—that of light. Space is where light can unfold and make what exists visible. In this painting one has the feeling that the light is about to condense into crystals—certainly the space here tends toward a crystalline structure.

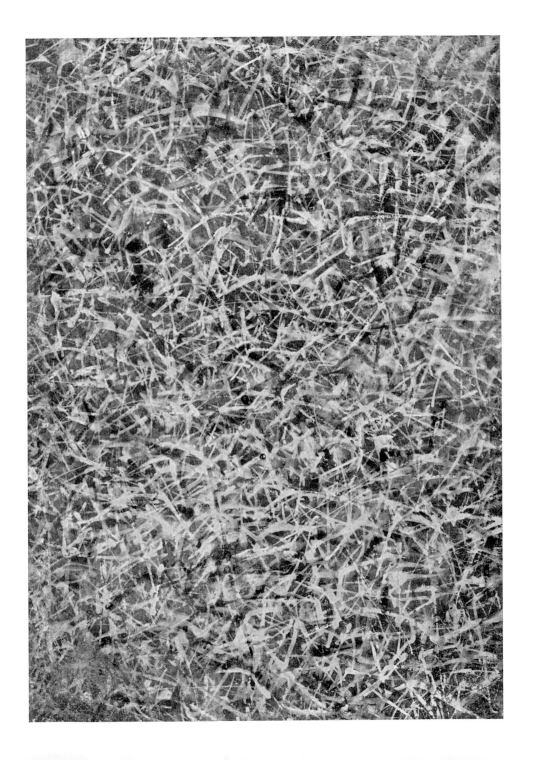

Claws of Orion. 1963

Here we have another picture of the starry heavens: the hands of Orion, who made the whole sky subject to himself. But at the same time it is a picture of the earth, for in the contemplation of a puddle of water, a bit of forest floor, or a length of muddy road the wise man can also see the clouds, the fields of stars, the nebulae in intergalactic space. This painting has no enclosing frame, and no drawing of characters to hold the surging space together. The red of the stars, light-years away, is at the same time quite close; it is embedded in the brown of passing veils of clouds, which is also the brown of this earth.

Calligraphic Dance. 1963

Tobey likes to experiment, to try new techniques, new materials, to explore his inner laws by playing with them, "just to amuse myself." As Kurt Schwitters was in one way, Tobey in his own way is convinced that the artist has the right to use all the materials that are visible to the eye and all available tools in the making of a picture. He might wish to add: As long as such media are capable of being transformed into spiritual expression. Here he has used a type of quick-drying glue which forces the hand to rapid motion. One draws spontaneously with it, or not at all. The result is reminiscent of the abstract hunting scenes in Stone Age caves. Spontaneity of the artist's gesture bridges millenniums.

The Sea. 1964

The same technique used in *Calligraphic Dance* here results in an entirely different effect—painting instead of callig-raphy. The sea. One senses the waves, the current, the raging, tumbling floodtide. Yet in the movement of the water, so it seems to us, there is also the gesture of the Japanese actor, as seen in the woodcuts of Sharaku, Utamaro, and others—the wild, frightening gestures of raging men. Perhaps this picture is the great dance of the *no* play, nature represented through the medium of man. An actor, at the climax of the production, must represent the sea, the raging of the flood, the crashing of breakers, the ebbtide. In a furious dance he transcends himself and *becomes* the sea. In a trance the audience follows his gestures—the waves of the sea, the arms of the ocean. Tobey's vision of this sea-dance is a masterpiece.

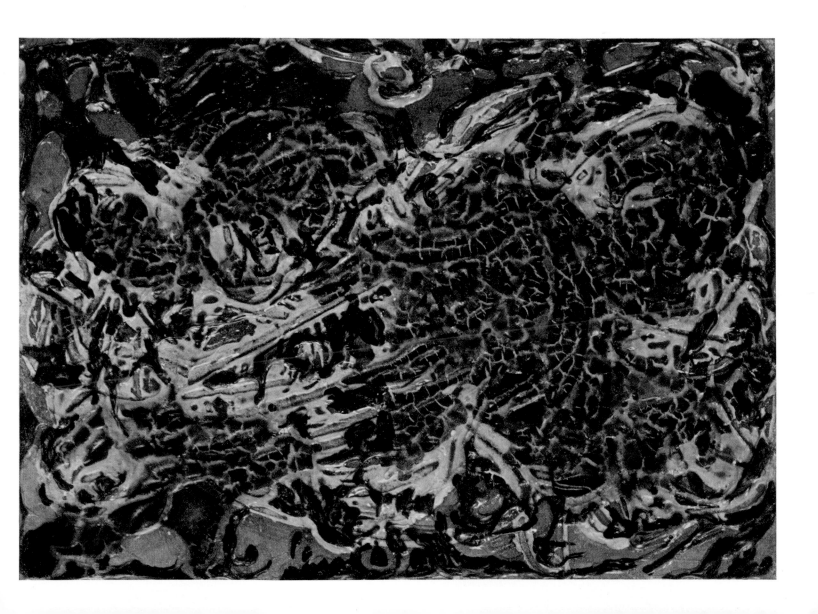

Biography

1890   Mark Tobey is born in Centerville, Wisconsin, on December 11, the youngest of four children of George Baker Tobey, a carpenter, housebuilder, and farmer, and his wife, Emma Jane (Cleveland) Tobey.

1893   The family moves to land near Jacksonville, Tennessee.

1894   The family moves to Trempealeau, Wisconsin. Trempealeau, situated on the Mississippi River, at that time had about 600 inhabitants. Here Mark Tobey spent his childhood and early youth. He went to the village school and attended church and Sunday school regularly (his parents were Congregationalists). His spare time he spent swimming, fishing, visiting Indian villages, and playing in the woods. In many of the paintings done in his twenties, and indirectly also in many later ones, there are lively memories of the Midwest.

1906   The family moves to Hammond, Indiana, where Mark goes to high school. He is an erratic student, especially interested in nature study, botany, and zoology. His love of art awakens, and on Saturdays he travels twelve miles to classes at the Art Institute of Chicago, to learn the techniques of watercolor and oil painting.

1909   The family moves to Chicago. Because of his father's illness, Mark gives up his art studies, leaves high school, and looks for a job. He tries to become a technical draftsman in the Northern Steel Works, like his brother Leon (born 1880). He is as unsuccessful in this as in a number of other professions he attempts. Finally he becomes an errand boy in a fashion design studio. Here his talent for drawing is discovered and he becomes a fashion illustrator. Becomes interested in Italian Renaissance art and in such painters as Hals, Sargent, Sorolla, and Zuloaga. Studies the work of commercial artists and Art Nouveau.

1911   First stay in New York, where he lives in Greenwich Village and manages to earn a living as a fashion illustrator.

1912	Returns to Chicago, still as a fashion illustrator.
1913	Sees the famous "Armory Show" at the Art Institute of Chicago, but is not much interested.
1913–17	Moves back and forth between New York and Chicago, continuing his studies on his own. Has some success drawing portraits in charcoal.
1917	First one-man show of portraits at the Knoedler Gallery in New York; then gives up portraiture for a while and goes into interior decorating, because it gives him more freedom.
1918	Poses for portrait painter Juliet Thompson, who introduces him to the Bahai World Faith, a creed of religious universalism with an optimistic outlook. He becomes a convert.
1918–22	Sees work by William Blake at the Pierpont Morgan Library in New York. Visits Marcel Duchamp. Portraits by Tobey appear in *The New York Times*. Draws Negro dancers in Harlem, and scenes from burlesque and vaudeville. After a marriage that lasts only a year, Tobey goes to Seattle.
1922–25	In Seattle he teaches painting at the Cornish School. His methods, which he calls "ideographic," are unconventional and motivated only by his love of art. His approach stresses the personal experiences of each student and of the teacher, rather than theoretical principles. He discovers Cubism, Japanese woodcuts, and American Indian art, and becomes a collector of the painting, weaving, and carving of the Tlinkit and Haida Indians of the Pacific Northwest. In a work like *Drums, Indians and the Word of God* (p. 30) one can readily see the influence of this Indian art on his own. Now he meets Teng Kwei, a Chinese student at the University of Washington, an encounter which is to be, next to his study of Bahaism, of the most profound significance in his life. From Kwei he learns the techniques of Far Eastern painting—its spirituality and its brushwork, calligraphy, and methods of com-

78

position. As Tobey expresses it later: "If our West Coast had been open to aesthetic influence from Asia, as the East Coast was to Europe, what a rich nation we would be!" To him, Seattle becomes the gateway to the Orient.

1925–26	Goes to Europe in June, and stays in Paris. Spends part of the winter in Châteaudun, near Chartres. Travels to Barcelona, Greece, Istanbul, and Beirut with friends in January, then makes a pilgrimage to the tombs of Bahaullah in Akká and Abdul-Bahá in Haifa. Becomes interested in Persian and Arabic calligraphy. Returns to Paris in February.
1927	Returns to Seattle.
1927–29	Lives intermittently in Seattle, Chicago, and in New York, where he meets Teng Kwei again.
1929	One-man show at Romany Marie's Café Gallery in New York. Alfred H. Barr sees his work and accepts several pictures for the exhibition, "Painting and Sculpture by Living Americans", at the Museum of Modern Art.
1930	Tobey accepts an invitation to teach at Dartington Hall, a progressive school in Devonshire, and moves to England.
1931	Trip to Mexico.
1931–38	Tobey is resident artist at Dartington Hall. He meets Pearl S. Buck, Aldous Huxley, Arthur Waley, Rabindranath Tagore, and Uday Shankar, who also teach there for shorter or longer periods, and who are all devoted to a fusion of East and West.
1933	Paints *Cirque d'Hiver* (p. 17).
1934	Travels to Japan, Ceylon, Hongkong, and to Shanghai, where he stays with Teng Kwei and his family. In Japan he sees the traditional *no* drama, Kabuki dancing, and Ikebana flower arranging. He spends a month in the seclusion of a Zen monastery in Kyoto, where he studies Zen and calligraphy, meditates, and writes poetry. In Japan his work receives the final "calligraphic

impulse," which leads to the "white writings" and to his awareness that he belongs as much to the East as to the West. In June, in a San Francisco hotel room, he paints the series "The Animal World Under Moonlight," in which the forms of the animals are rendered almost calligraphically.

1935–36   Returns to Seattle. First one-man museum exhibition (Seattle Art Museum). Returns to Dartington Hall via New York. There he paints *Broadway Norm*, *Broadway* (p. 18), and *Welcome Hero*, in three consecutive nights, initiating with these paintings the style known as "white writing."

1938   After a short stay in New York he returns to Seattle, where he teaches painting in his studio.

1940   During the forties he develops his "white writing." He wins the Baker Memorial Award in the Northwest Annual Exhibition, Seattle Art Museum. Studies music (flute and piano).

1942   His painting, *Broadway* (p. 18), is entered in the exhibition "Artists for Victory" at the Metropolitan Museum of Art, and wins a purchase prize.

1944   One-man exhibition at the Willard Gallery in New York, which exhibits his work regularly thereafter. The beginnings of his national reputation.

1952   A film, *Mark Tobey: Artist*, is shown at film festivals in Venice and Edinburgh.

1954   Travels to Sweden to see his friend Pehr Hallsten, a Swedish-American scholar and painter. Exhibition at the Otto Seligman Gallery in Seattle.

1955   Travels to Paris, England, and Basel, and to Berne to see the "Tendances Actuelles" exhibition at the Kunsthalle. First one-man show in Europe, at the Galerie Jeanne Bucher, Paris. The beginnings of his international reputation.

1956   Tobey, in Seattle, can now live from his painting alone. Awarded the United States National Prize in the Guggenheim International Award. Elected to the National Institute of Arts and Letters.

1957   Concentrates on Japanese ink painting (*sumi*).

1958   Wins first prize for painting at the Venice Biennale. Travels to Europe in July: to England, Italy, Switzerland. Visits the World's Fair in Brussels. Returns to New York in October.

1959   Paints a mural for the Washington State Library in Seattle, and spends the summer in Paris.

1960   Settles in Basel, where the humanistic tradition conforms to his own thinking. He rents a house in the suburb of St. Alban, where he lives with Pehr Hallsten and his secretary and translator, Mark Ritter. Makes contact with the Galerie Beyeler. Is elected a member of the American Academy of Arts and Sciences, but declines the membership. In September he takes part in the Congress of the International Association of Plastic Arts, in Vienna, the subject of which is "Orient—Occident."

1961   Retrospective show at the Musée des Arts Décoratifs in Paris (Palais du Louvre, Pavillon de Marsan).

1962   Retrospective show at the Museum of Modern Art, New York, then at the Cleveland Museum of Art and at the Institute of Chicago. Returns to New York with Pehr Hallsten; summers in Seattle; then returns to Basel.

1963   Spring in Seattle.

1964–66   In Basel.

Selected Bibliography

Monographs

Choay, Françoise. *Mark Tobey*, Paris, Fernand Hazan, 1961
Roberts, Colette. *Tobey*, Paris, Le Musée de Poche, 1959. English edition: New York, Grove Press, 1960
Seitz, William C. *Mark Tobey*, New York, Museum of Modern Art, 1962

Texts by Tobey (arranged chronologically)

"Artist's Mind at Work," *Limited Edition*, December 1945 [Statement]
"Reminiscense and Reverie," *Magazine of Art*, October 1951
"Japanese Traditions and American Art," *College Art Journal*, Fall, 1958
Kuh, Katherine. "The Painters Meets the Critic," *Saturday Review*, July 2, 1960 [Interview]
Chevalier, Denys. "Une journée avec Mark Tobey," *Aujour-d'hui*, October 1961 [Interview]

Selected Articles on Tobey

Alvard, Julien. "Tobey," *Cimaise*, May 1965
Ashton, Dore. "Mark Tobey et la rondeur parfaite," *XXe Siècle*, May-June 1959
Breuning, Margaret. "World's Imprints on Seattle's Mark Tobey," *Art Digest*, October 1951
Courtois, Michel. "Mark Tobey—des pictogrammes indiens à l'écriture blanche," *Cahiers du Musée de Poche*, March 1959
Flanner, Janet. "Sage from Wisconsin," *Selective Eye*, 1955
Kochnitzky, Léon. "Mark Tobey," *Quadrum*, 1957
Oeri, Georgine. "Tobey and Rothko," *Baltimore Museum of Art News*, Winter 1960

Ragon, Michel. "A 70 ans Tobey est révélé par Paris," *Arts* (Paris), October 18–24, 1961

Restany, Pierre. "Mark Tobey," *Cimaise*, March–April 1958

Rexroth, Kenneth. "Mark Tobey of Seattle, Wash.," *Art News*, May 1951

Rotzler, Willy. "Mark Tobey," *DU*, August 1963

Schulz, Phoebe. "Mark Tobey," *Das Kunstwerk*, September 1957

Wiegand, Charmion von. "The Vision of Mark Tobey," *Arts* (New York), September 1959

Zervos, Christian. "Mark Tobey," *Cahiers d'Art*, 1954

Catalogues (arranged chronologically)

Portland Art Museum. Paintings by Mark Tobey. Portland, Oregon, 1945 [Circulated to San Francisco Art Museum, Arts Club of Chicago, Detroit Institute of Arts]

Whitney Museum of American Art. Mark Tobey. Retrospective exhibition. New York, 1951

Museum of Modern Art. International Council. Lipton, Rothko, Smith, Tobey. XXIX Biennale, Venice, 1958. "Mark Tobey," by Frank O'Hara

Seattle Art Museum. Mark Tobey: a retrospective exhibition from Northwest Collections. Seattle, Washington, 1959 [Circulated to Portland, Colorado Springs, Pasadena, San Francisco]

Kunsthalle, Mannheim. "Mark Tobey," by Heinz Fuchs, 1961

Galerie Beyeler. "Mark Tobey," by Julia and Lyonel Feininger. Basel, 1961

Musée des Arts Décoratifs. Mark Tobey. Paris, 1961 [Also shown at The Whitechapel Gallery, London, 1962]

Konstsalongen Samlaren, Stockholm, and Goteborgs Konstmuseum, Goteborg. "Tobey," by Julien Alvard, François Mathey, and Alfred Westholm. 1962

Galerie Beyeler. Arp, Bissier, Nicholson, Tobey. Basel, October 1963